WASPI Women

A Fight for Pension Justice and Equality

Kingsley Freeman

Table of content

Introduction

Part 1: The Roots of the Crisis

Part 2: The Impact on WASPI Women

Part 3: The Struggle for Justice

Part 4: Wider Implications of Pension Inequality

Part 5: The Path Forward

Conclusion

Introduction

The letter came folded crisply, wedged between flyers and bills, slipping unnoticed onto doormats across Britain. For many women born in the 1950s, it wasn't the arrival of the envelope that struck a note of dread it was what lay inside. A few lines of carefully worded bureaucratic jargon that read as though written by someone who'd never stood in their shoes, never known a day of worry over an unpaid bill or an empty fridge.

Margaret found hers late on a Tuesday afternoon. She was sifting through post after a day of work, the tips of her fingers smudged with flour from the bakery where she spent hours kneading and shaping dough. Her bones ached, her shoes pinched at the corners of her feet, and the long walk home had left her breath heavy in her chest. At 59, Margaret had counted down the years until she could hang up her apron, finally rest, and allow herself a semblance of peace after decades of sacrifice.

Her fingers tore at the corner of the envelope, her mind already elsewhere perhaps on what little food she'd scrape together for dinner or the call she'd promised to her grown daughter later that night. Her eyes skimmed the lines of text, struggling for comprehension. The paper rustled in her hands as the words came into focus.

"Changes to the state pension age mean that women born between 1950 and 1955 will not receive their pensions until the age of 65. This decision is in line with government policy changes..."

She read it again, slower this time, as if the meaning would change. Her heart sank, the paper growing heavier in her hands. Her pension something she'd worked for, something promised, a silent assurance that her labor had not been in vain had been pushed further out of reach. The age had shifted. Sixty-five.

Margaret sat down, her body folding into the worn armchair in her living room. Her palms trembled. She thought of the bakery of the mornings spent in the cold dark, walking to open the shop before the rest of the street stirred awake. She thought of the aches in her wrists, the persistent pain in her knees that didn't let her sleep most nights. How much more could she give?

Across Britain, in places like Birmingham, Manchester, Glasgow, and Brighton, millions of women faced the same hollow realization. For many of them, this change was not simply a delay in payments it was an undoing of everything they'd planned for, a cruel rewriting of their futures.

In cramped kitchens, women sat at small tables covered in checkered clothes, calculators and papers spread across the surface as they tried to make the math work. What did two, three, or five extra years of waiting mean? It meant continuing in jobs that wore their bodies down like sandpaper against stone. It meant late nights cleaning offices or waking up before dawn to stand behind counters.

Carol, a former nurse who'd spent decades lifting patients out of beds, changing dressings, and holding the hands of strangers during their final hours, sat with her husband at their kitchen table, the news replaying on the television in the background. The broadcaster spoke of "policy fairness," his voice detached and smooth, but Carol barely heard him.

"I can't do it, Frank," she whispered. Her hands clutched a steaming mug of tea, the heat barely warming her fingertips. "I just can't lift another person out of a bed. My back had it. My knees too."

Her husband didn't reply at first. His face was fixed, his brow heavy. He knew. Carol had come home limping more nights than not. She'd smiled through the pain, saying it was just "a little catch," but he'd seen her wince when climbing the stairs.

"What choice do we have?" Frank finally muttered, his words like gravel tumbling out.

For women like Carol, the thought of carrying on wasn't just unfair it was impossible. Their bodies had already paid the price. Every crease in their skin, every arthritic joint, every sleepless night spent worrying about unpaid gas bills were receipts for a lifetime spent working, giving, and holding up homes, families, and entire communities.

But now they were being told to wait longer, to do more.
In towns battered by factory closures and dwindling opportunities, the pension delay hit hardest. Women who'd raised children through strikes, through recessions, and through years of political promises now found themselves betrayed. They'd been daughters of war-time parents, growing up in homes where every

penny was stretched, every scrap of fabric reused. They carried those lessons into adulthood, working as cleaners, shop assistants, caretakers, and seamstresses.

Christine worked in a textile mill for more than 30 years, the hum of machinery her constant companion. She learned to move quickly, hands steady as they fed fabric through the rollers. When the factory shut down in the early 2000s, Christine was just shy of 50. She scraped by on temporary jobs, cutting back on groceries, taking in sewing work from neighbors. She'd pinned her hopes on her pension as her "ticket out" a small cushion that would allow her to rest.

The letter that came for her was no different from Margaret's or Carol's. It was written in cold ink and without apology. When she told her sister about it, her voice cracked as she tried to hold herself together.

"They act like we've done nothing," Christine said, her words clipped, heavy with anger she could barely contain. "They've taken everything we've given, and now they want us to give more."

For some, the news carried another, more sinister cost loneliness. Women who were widowed, divorced, or caring for sick relatives had already been struggling in silence. Without the pension they'd counted on, isolation deepened. Bills went unpaid, meals were skipped, and friendships dissolved under the weight of worry.

Brenda, who lived alone in a small flat in Liverpool, began selling bits of furniture to make rent. "I'll be fine," she told her son over the phone, masking the exhaustion in her voice. "I'll figure it out." She never told him how she spent evenings in the dark to save on electricity, or how the fridge rattled emptily most weeks.
Her pension had been her safety net. Without it, every day felt like walking a tightrope, each step more precarious than the last.

The government's justification was rooted in policy and fairness. Raising the pension age for women to align with men's was framed as equality—a move toward balance. But for the women born in the 1950s, who were rarely given equal opportunities or wages, the word "fair" tasted bitter. They had spent years working longer hours for less pay. They'd stayed home to raise children, sacrificing career prospects to hold families together. Now, when it was finally their turn to rest, they were told they would have to wait.

For them, this wasn't equality it was punishment for the paths life had forced them to take.

The letters kept coming. The news spread. Women gathered in living rooms, at cafés, in community halls, sharing their stories like wounds that needed airing. The WASPI campaign was born not out of anger alone but out of survival. Voices rose together, demanding to be heard, refusing to be forgotten.

The women of the 1950s were not just a generation they were the backbone of their country, the quiet architects of its progress. Their hands had worked, lifted, healed, and held without complaint. Now, they were being left behind.

And they would not accept it quietly.

Part 1: The Roots of the Crisis

The concept of a state pension in the United Kingdom began as a lifeline a government promise that after decades of labor, citizens could rest, knowing their country would provide a safety net. But pensions were never born out of generosity; they were forged in the fires of social necessity, shaped by poverty, wars, and changing demographics.

To understand the pension system is to understand a compact between a nation and its people. Workers contribute over a lifetime, paying into National Insurance as they navigate careers filled with sweat and sacrifice. The reward, at the end of that journey, is the state pension a modest income that allows people to live with dignity after their working years are behind them.

But pensions were never designed to be luxurious. In cramped flats and terraced houses, pensioners live on figures that just barely keep the lights on. For decades, women often caregivers, often paid less relied on this promise even more than their male counterparts.

The History of the State Pension and Its Role in Society

The UK's state pension system took its first breath in 1908 under the Old Age Pensions Act. Introduced to combat extreme poverty among the elderly, the system paid a small sum to men and women over the age of 70. But it came with strict conditions only those who'd led lives deemed "honorable" were eligible. Paupers, habitual drinkers, and those who hadn't worked consistently were excluded.

By the time World War II tore through Europe, Britain's working-class families were already weighed down by hardship. Young men fought and died on foreign soil while women carried the country on their shoulders working in factories, farming the fields, and raising families alone.

After the war, the Beveridge Report of 1942 laid out the blueprint for the modern welfare state, including pensions as a cornerstone of its vision. It promised security from "cradle to grave" a guarantee that hard work would one day be rewarded with dignity.

For post-war generations, particularly those born in the 1950s, the state pension was more than financial support; it was woven into the fabric of their lives. Women took on roles as mothers, wives, and workers, many navigating jobs with wages far beneath their male colleagues'. They trusted the pension system to bridge the gap, offering reassurance that their sacrifices would be acknowledged when the time came.

The Decision to Raise the Pension Age for Women

In the early 1990s, the UK government found itself staring at a future it hadn't planned for. People were living longer, healthier lives—an unexpected blessing that carried with it financial strain. The state pension, once sufficient for a population with shorter life expectancies, was becoming unsustainable. Reform was inevitable.

The solution came in the form of the 1995 Pension Act, a policy that raised the state pension age for women from 60 to 65, aligning it with men. On paper, the reasoning was simple: equality. Europe was pushing for gender parity in retirement laws, and the UK was under pressure to comply. Officials spoke of fairness and fiscal responsibility, presenting the changes as a necessary modernization.

But behind the white papers and parliamentary debates lay a truth that went unspoken—this decision would disproportionately affect women, particularly those born in the 1950s. They had grown up in an era when "equality" was still a distant dream. Most left school early, finding jobs in factories, shops, and offices while juggling the unpaid labor of home life. Few had access to private pensions or savings plans that would cushion the blow of a delayed state pension.

The government insisted that women would have time to adjust, but the whispers of change didn't reach the ears of those most affected. Notices were buried in legal jargon, printed in documents few ever saw. The message was delivered quietly, as if hiding behind the curtain of policy would soften its impact.

The 1995 Act wasn't just a policy shift it was a seismic change with ripple effects that would stretch for decades. For women approaching retirement, the change meant recalibrating their lives with little warning. Retirement plans dissolved. Budgets tightened. Dreams of finally resting were replaced by the grim realization that they'd need to carry on often in jobs that demanded more than their aging bodies could give.

ary, a former cleaner from Leeds, remembers the day she realized she'd have to keep working past 60. She had dreamed of retiring quietly, spending her mornings sipping tea in the garden she'd neglected for years. Instead, she found herself kneeling on cold linoleum floors, scrubbing at stains in strangers' kitchens.

"My body's breaking," she whispered to her friend one afternoon, her voice low, her breath labored. "But they don't care, do they?"

Women like Mary, who had given everything to their families and employers, now felt abandoned. The promise they'd clung to that the state pension would catch them had been snatched away.

The Silent Changes of 2011

In 2011, the government delivered the final blow. Under the guise of fiscal urgency, the coalition government accelerated the pension age increases, shortening the timeline yet again. Women who had already been blindsided by the 1995 Act now found themselves pushed even further back, with some forced to wait an additional 18 months to two years for their pensions.

The announcement came like a quiet storm, sweeping through living rooms and kitchens where women listened to news bulletins with stunned disbelief. Many had made their peace with working longer, but the acceleration undid whatever fragile plans they'd managed to piece together.

For Christine, a former librarian from Bristol, the news felt like betrayal layered upon betrayal. Her face crumpled as she listened to the announcement on the radio. "How much more are they going to take?" she murmured, her voice breaking.

How Communication Failures Amplified the Problem

The failure to communicate these changes effectively deepened the crisis. Official notifications were sparse, and many women received no formal warning at all. Some discovered the changes only when they applied for their pensions, their shock giving way to anger and confusion.

Pamela, a mother of three who'd worked as a carer for much of her life, didn't find out until she visited her local Jobcentre to discuss her pension. The clerk had glanced at her paperwork, then said bluntly, "You're not eligible until you're 66 now."

Pamela blinked, stunned. "But I'm 60," she replied.

"Doesn't matter. They've changed it."

The explanation was cold and clinical, devoid of apology. Pamela's mind reeled. She thought of the years she'd spent caring for others her parents, her husband when he fell ill and the part-time jobs she'd picked up along the way. There was no time to save, no time to plan. Now, she would have to carry on working, though her back ached every day and her hands were stiff with arthritis.

"How can they do this to us?" she asked later, her voice a whisper.

The silence that followed spoke volumes.

Part 2: The Impact on WASPI Women

The shock did not come all at once it crept into kitchens, workplaces, and homes like an unwelcome guest. For the women born in the 1950s, the realization of what had been taken from them often began with a letter or a conversation at the local Jobcentre.

Patricia, a widow from Birmingham, had spent her life juggling work and family. Her days started before sunrise, preparing her three children for school, then heading to her job as a cleaner at a local primary school. By the time she got home, the day's demands were far from over dinner had to be made, uniforms washed, and bills balanced.

She had always looked ahead to her retirement as a time to finally exhale. But that hope unraveled one cold morning when she opened a letter from the Department for Work and

Pensions. She scanned the lines quickly, her heart sinking with every word. Her pension, the safety net she had relied on, would not be there at 60. She would have to wait another six years.

Her first thought wasn't about herself but her body her back that ached from decades of scrubbing floors, her knees that had screamed in protest every time she climbed stairs. How could she possibly go on?

In small towns and bustling cities, the stories were the same. Women like Patricia faced more than just disappointment they faced the sudden, brutal reality of carrying burdens they thought they'd finally set down.

Margaret, a former factory worker, watched as her savings dwindled. She had planned meticulously for her retirement, but the delayed pension forced her to dip into the small pot she'd scraped together. Each withdrawal felt like a betrayal of the promises she had built her life around.

"I did everything right," she said, her voice breaking during a community meeting organized by the WASPI campaign. "I worked. I saved. And now, it's not enough."

For others, the health challenges were insurmountable. Elizabeth, who had spent decades on her feet as a waitress, was diagnosed with chronic fatigue syndrome at 59. Her doctor warned her to slow down, but slowing down wasn't an option. With no pension to fall back on, she pushed through each shift, collapsing into bed at the end of the day, her body too drained to move.

The Emotional Toll

The financial struggles were only one side of the coin. For many women, the pension changes shattered their trust in the very system they had supported all their lives. Anxiety became a constant companion, its weight pressing down in moments of silence.

Helen, a retired shop assistant, described the sleepless nights she endured after learning she would need to continue working. "It's not just the money," she explained during a WASPI support group meeting. "It's the fear fear that I won't be able to make it, fear that I'll lose everything before I even get there."
Despair, too, crept into their lives. Karen, a retired librarian, admitted to her friends that she sometimes felt like giving up. Her modest savings had been drained, and her part-time work barely covered her rent. She stared at eviction notices, her hands trembling, wondering how things had come to this.

Case Studies: Women Forced into Hardship and Debt
Christine's story stood out among the WASPI campaign's case studies. A widow from Glasgow, Christine had worked as a seamstress for nearly 40 years. When her pension age was extended, she was forced to take out loans to make ends meet. The interest mounted quickly, and soon, she found herself spiraling into debt.

"I used to take pride in never owing anyone anything," she said during a WASPI rally, her voice trembling with frustration. "Now, I can't even afford to heat my flat."

Her words resonated with others in the crowd. For many, debt became an unavoidable reality as they scrambled to cover basic expenses. Credit cards, payday loans, and overdrafts became lifelines, pulling them further into financial uncertainty.

The Campaign is Born

The anger and frustration that simmered in living rooms and community halls eventually boiled over into action. In 2015, a group of women came together to form the Women Against State Pension Inequality (WASPI) campaign. Their goal was simple but ambitious: to demand justice for the millions of women whose lives had been upended by the pension changes.

The first WASPI meeting was held in a small community center in Manchester. Women from all walks of life filled the room, their faces etched with determination. They shared stories of hardship and betrayal, their voices growing louder with each tale.

"We won't be ignored," one woman declared, her words sparking applause.

Early Activism, Rallies, and the Fight for Awareness

The WASPI campaign quickly gained momentum. Women donned purple sashes and marched through the streets of London, holding banners that read: "We Paid In, You Pay Out!" Their voices echoed through the corridors of power, demanding recognition and reparations.

Social media became a powerful tool for the campaign. WASPI's online presence grew rapidly, with thousands of women sharing their stories and rallying support. Petitions gained hundreds of thousands of signatures, and politicians began to take notice.

The campaign wasn't without its challenges. Critics dismissed their demands as unrealistic, while others argued that the government's hands were tied by budget constraints. But the WASPI women refused to back down.

Part 3: The Struggle for Justice

Administrative Failures and Miscommunication Exposed

The damning words of the Parliamentary and Health Service Ombudsman landed like a thunderclap in 2021. For the women who had spent years battling for recognition, the findings were both vindication and a bitter reminder of the negligence that had shattered their lives. The report laid bare the government's administrative failures, specifically the Department for Work and Pensions' (DWP) failure to adequately communicate the changes to the state pension age.

In a quiet corner of her home in Nottingham, Susan, a 64-year-old former nurse, sat with a copy of the report in her hands. Her glasses perched on her nose, she read the lines slowly, her pulse quickening as the weight of the findings sank in. "The DWP failed to act promptly to inform women about the changes. This was maladministration."

Her breath caught in her throat. Those words maladministration felt like a lifeline, a validation of everything she and thousands of others had endured. Yet, anger simmered beneath her relief. The report confirmed what they had known all along: the government had let them down, not through intention, but through carelessness, through a system that treated lives like entries in a spreadsheet.

The Ombudsman's investigation revealed that, for years, letters about the pension age changes had either been delayed or not sent at all. Women born between 1950 and 1955 had no idea their retirement plans were in jeopardy until it was too late.

Patricia, a 63-year-old single mother, was one of the many who never received notification. "I never got a letter. Not one," she said during a WASPI meeting, her voice trembling. "I found out when I applied for my pension. They told me I had another six years to go. I thought it was a mistake how could they not tell me?"

For Patricia and others like her, the Ombudsman's findings were a stark reminder of the chaos that had upended their lives. The maladministration wasn't just a bureaucratic failure it was a betrayal of trust.

The Ombudsman didn't stop at highlighting failures. It went further, recommending compensation for the women affected. The suggested amounts ranging from £1,000 to £2,950 per woman were a fraction of what many had lost, but they carried symbolic weight. For the WASPI women, the call for compensation represented acknowledgment, a public admission that the system had wronged them.

Yet, for many, the numbers felt inadequate. Elizabeth, a retired care worker from Manchester, scoffed at the suggested figure when she read it in the news. "£2,950? That's not even close to what I've lost. They've taken years from me. How do you put a price on that?"

Despite these frustrations, the fight for compensation became a rallying cry. WASPI leaders saw it as a crucial step toward justice, a way to hold the government accountable for the lives disrupted by its negligence.

Political Roadblocks and Resistance

The road to justice, however, was anything but smooth. Successive UK governments had little appetite for addressing the WASPI crisis. Politicians spoke in measured tones, offering sympathy but little action. Their responses often boiled down to one stark truth: money. Compensation for the estimated 3.8 million women affected would cost billions a figure no government was willing to shoulder.

In Westminster, the issue became a political hot potato. Prime Minister after Prime Minister sidestepped the growing anger, framing the changes as necessary adjustments to an aging population. Behind closed doors, Treasury officials whispered about the budget deficit, warning against setting precedents that could spark further claims.

For the WASPI women, these excuses felt like salt in the wound. "They've got money when it suits them," muttered Brenda, a 66-year-old former shopkeeper from Liverpool. "Billions for banks when they need bailing out, but nothing for us? We're not asking for a handout we're asking for what's fair."

Why the Compensation Debate Divided the Nation

Public opinion on the WASPI issue remained divided. On one side were those who sympathized deeply with the women's plight, recognizing the injustice of a system that had failed to communicate life-altering changes. On the other were critics who argued that the changes were fair and that compensation was an unnecessary burden on taxpayers.

Tabloid headlines often reflected this divide. Some publications ran sympathetic features, highlighting the stories of women forced into poverty and despair. Others framed the campaign as unrealistic, painting the WASPI women as unwilling to adapt to modern realities.

The debate reached a fever pitch in 2024 when the government formally rejected the Ombudsman's compensation recommendations. Work and Pensions Secretary Liz Kendall defended the decision, citing fairness to taxpayers and financial constraints. Her statement was clinical, her tone devoid of emotion. "While we acknowledge the difficulties faced by the women affected, compensation on this scale is neither affordable nor justifiable."

The WASPI community erupted. Protests broke out in cities across the UK, with women marching through the streets in their signature purple sashes. Signs reading "Fairness, Not Excuses" bobbed above the crowds as chants of

"We paid in, you pay out!" echoed through Westminster.

The Fight in the Courts and Parliament

The WASPI movement responded to political resistance with renewed determination, taking their fight to the courts and Parliament. Petitions gathered millions of signatures, forcing debates in the House of Commons. Women traveled from across the country to witness the hearings, their presence a quiet reminder of the human cost behind the statistics.

In one such hearing, Margaret, a retired teacher, stood before a packed room, her hands trembling slightly as she gripped the edges of the podium. She recounted how she'd worked for 40 years, planning meticulously for her retirement, only to be blindsided by the changes. "I've given everything to this country," she said, her voice steady despite the emotion cracking at its edges. "Now, when I need help, I'm told to wait. How is that fair?"Her words hung in the air, met with solemn nods from some MPs and guarded expressions from others.

Meanwhile, legal challenges mounted. In 2019, a group of women filed a judicial review against the DWP, arguing that the pension changes were discriminatory. The case drew widespread attention, with news cameras capturing images of the plaintiffs standing outside the courthouse, their faces resolute.

Though the courts ultimately ruled against the WASPI women, the case served as a rallying point, galvanizing support and keeping the issue in the public eye.

Women's Stories as Evidence: A Fight for Recognition

Throughout the struggle, the stories of individual women became the beating heart of the campaign. Each narrative, though unique, shared common threads of loss, betrayal, and resilience.

Susan, a 67-year-old grandmother from Wales, spoke during a public inquiry about how the pension changes had forced her to sell her home. "I had no choice," she explained, her voice cracking. "I couldn't afford the mortgage anymore. I live with my daughter now, and as much as I love her, it's not the life I planned for."

Her testimony was met with murmurs of sympathy, but sympathy wasn't enough. For the WASPI women, recognition meant action legislation, compensation, and a public acknowledgment of the wrongs they had endured.

Part 4: Wider Implications of Pension Inequality

How Gender and Economic Disparities
Amplified the Impact

In the quiet hours of the morning, before the city stirred awake, Patricia sat at her kitchen table with her fingers wrapped tightly around a chipped mug. The weight of years hung heavily on her shoulders. She had worked since she was 16, first in a textile factory, then as a school cleaner. The work was relentless, and the pay had barely covered the essentials. Now, at 62, she faced the grim reality that her pension was still years away, leaving her to scrape by on odd jobs and small savings that dwindled faster than she could replenish them.

Patricia's story wasn't unique. It was shared by millions of women across the UK who had faced a lifetime of systemic inequality. For decades, women had been paid less than men for the same work, often forced into lower-paying jobs or part-time roles due to caregiving responsibilities. The 1950s-born women were among the first to enter the workforce en masse, but they were also the first to confront its limitations.

In the 1970s, as the Equal Pay Act came into effect, many women like Patricia were optimistic that the gap between men's and women's wages would close. But progress was slow, and the damage was already done. By the time the pension age changes were announced, these women were already at a disadvantage. Most had no private pensions or savings to fall back on, relying entirely on the state pension to carry them through retirement.

For women who had taken time off to raise children or care for elderly relatives, the disparities were even more pronounced. Susan, a widow from Glasgow, had spent years looking after her mother and later her husband, who had suffered a stroke. She worked part-time when she could, cleaning offices in the evenings after putting her children to bed.

"I didn't think about pensions back then," she explained during a WASPI rally. "I was just trying to keep food on the table. The state pension was supposed to be there for people like me people who gave everything they could, even if it wasn't enough to save."

For many women, the delayed pension age wasn't just an inconvenience it was the breaking point of a lifetime spent fighting against a system that had never been designed for them.

A Broader Look at Women's Financial Vulnerability

The pension crisis shone a harsh light on a broader issue: women's financial vulnerability. Across the UK, women were more likely to live in poverty than men, particularly in older age. They were less likely to own property, more likely to have gaps in their employment history, and more likely to take on unpaid labor.

Brenda, a 64-year-old former shop assistant, understood this all too well. After her divorce, she struggled to make ends meet. Her ex-husband had a pension from his years working in construction, but Brenda, who had spent much of her marriage raising their children, had nothing.

"I used to think we'd share everything," she said, her voice tinged with bitterness. "But when the marriage ended, so did my security. And now the government's taken away the one thing I had left to look forward to."

The issue extended beyond pensions. Women faced systemic barriers at every stage of their lives lower wages, limited career progression, and a disproportionate burden of unpaid care work. The pension inequality was merely the final blow, leaving many women feeling invisible and forgotten.

Global Pension Inequality

Similar Cases Around the World: Lessons from Other Countries

The UK was not alone in grappling with the complexities of pension inequality. Across the globe, women faced similar challenges, their stories echoing the frustrations of the WASPI women.

In the United States, for example, women received significantly lower Social Security benefits than men due to the same systemic factors: lower lifetime earnings and more time spent out of the workforce. For many American women, retirement wasn't a respite but a continuation of the financial struggles they had faced throughout their lives.

Maria, a retired schoolteacher in California, shared a story that mirrored Patricia's. After dedicating her career to teaching, she found herself struggling to make ends meet when her pension fell short of her expectations. "I thought I'd done everything right," she said during a public forum on pension reform. "But now I'm choosing between paying for my medication and paying my rent."

In countries like Germany and France, similar debates were unfolding. Women in both nations had protested changes to pension policies that disproportionately affected caregivers and part-time workers. In Germany, the introduction of a points-based pension system had widened the gap between men and women, leaving many women reliant on government subsidies to survive.

Even in countries with more progressive policies, such as Sweden, the issue persisted. While Sweden's pension system was lauded for its inclusivity, women still received lower payouts on average due to gendered income disparities.

A Shared Struggle for Economic Fairness

The global nature of pension inequality underscored a shared struggle for economic fairness. Women around the world were demanding more than just financial security they were demanding recognition of the contributions they had made to their families, their communities, and their countries.

The WASPI campaign became part of a larger movement, connecting with activists in other nations to share strategies and stories. International conferences on gender and pensions brought together voices from every corner of the globe, creating a united front against a system that had long ignored women's needs.

But the fight for fairness wasn't just about pensions. It was about dismantling the structures that had kept women economically vulnerable for generations. Activists pushed for policies that addressed pay equity, affordable childcare, and recognition of unpaid labor.

For Patricia and others like her, the knowledge that their struggle was part of something bigger provided a small measure of comfort. "We're not just fighting for ourselves," she said during a WASPI meeting. "We're fighting for the women who come after us. They deserve better than this."

Part 5: The Path Forward

The room buzzed with quiet intensity, the kind that precedes a defining moment. Women of all ages filled the seats, wearing purple sashes that had come to symbolize their shared struggle. Their faces were etched with determination, weathered by years of battle yet illuminated by a spark that refused to die. It was a rally organized by the WASPI (Women Against State Pension Inequality) campaign, and in every word spoken, every banner raised, there was a sense of history being written.

The WASPI campaign didn't begin with the intent to change the world. It began with letters sent in frustration, conversations over kitchen tables, and tears shed in the solitude of sleepless nights. But as the movement grew, so did its influence. What started as a cry for justice became something bigger a redefinition of activism for women's rights in the modern era.

Margaret, a retired teacher who had never attended a protest in her life, found herself standing at the front of a march in London, holding a placard that read, "Fairness for Women Born in the 1950s!" Her voice joined the chants that echoed down Whitehall, surprising even herself. "I never thought I'd be here," she said later, her cheeks flushed with the excitement of the day. "But when they take away your dignity, you have no choice but to fight back."

For many WASPI women, this was their first experience with organized activism. They weren't seasoned campaigners; they were mothers, grandmothers, widows, and wives, bound together by a shared sense of betrayal. Yet their passion and resilience turned them into a formidable force. Through marches, petitions, social media campaigns, and high-profile meetings with politicians, they made their voices impossible to ignore.

The legacy of WASPI extends beyond the immediate fight for pension equality. It inspired a new generation of activists, showing that it's never too late to stand up for what's right. Young women, watching their mothers and grandmothers take to the streets, saw the power of collective action firsthand.

The Stories That Inspired a Generation

What made the WASPI campaign resonate so deeply were the stories raw, personal, and impossible to dismiss. Each woman who stepped forward to share her experience became a thread in a larger narrative of resilience.

Christine's story, for example, became emblematic of the campaign's emotional core. A seamstress from Glasgow, she had worked tirelessly for over 40 years, stitching together garments in poorly lit factories for wages that barely kept her afloat. When she learned her pension had been delayed, she was forced to sell her home. Standing in front of a crowd of hundreds at a WASPI rally, she spoke through tears.

"I gave my whole life to this country," she said, her voice trembling but strong. "I wasn't asking for charity I was asking for what I earned. And they took it away."

Her words were met with applause that seemed to ripple through the crowd like a wave, carrying with it a renewed sense of purpose. Stories like Christine's put a human face on the crisis, turning abstract policy into a deeply personal issue that could not be ignored.

Pension Reform: What Needs to Change?

The WASPI movement may have begun as a reaction to a specific injustice, but it quickly became a broader call for reform. The pension system, as it stood, was riddled with inconsistencies and inequalities that extended far beyond the 1950s-born women. To fix it, advocates argued, required more than band-aid solutionsit demanded a complete overhaul.

At the heart of the proposed reforms were three principles: fairness, transparency, and equality. Fairness meant acknowledging the disproportionate impact of pension changes on women and addressing the systemic disparities that had compounded their struggles. Transparency meant ensuring that future policy changes were communicated clearly and in a timely manner, so no one else would be blindsided as the WASPI women had been. Equality meant recognizing and addressing the unique challenges faced by women in the workforce, from lower wages to unpaid caregiving responsibilities.

Policy experts and activists proposed specific measures, including:

Improved communication strategies to ensure pension changes are clearly conveyed to all affected parties.

Recognition of unpaid labor in the calculation of pension entitlements, particularly for women who took time off to raise children or care for relatives.

Flexible retirement options that allow individuals to access partial pensions if needed.

The WASPI campaign made it clear that these reforms weren't just about addressing past wrongs they were about building a more equitable future.

The Role of Governments, Advocacy, and Future Generations

The responsibility for pension reform ultimately lies with governments, but the role of advocacy groups like WASPI cannot be overstated. By keeping the issue in the public eye, they created a sense of urgency that policymakers could no longer ignore.

For future generations, the WASPI fight serves as a cautionary tale and a call to action. It highlights the importance of vigilance in holding governments accountable and the power of grassroots movements to drive change.

Hope, Resilience, and Solidarity

The fight for justice is far from over. While the WASPI campaign has achieved significant milestones drawing national and international attention to the issue of pension inequality the core demand for compensation remains unmet.

Yet, the women of WASPI refuse to give up. In community centers and online forums, they continue to strategize, organize, and push for change. Their resilience is a testament to the strength of collective action, a reminder that even in the face of seemingly insurmountable odds, progress is possible.

For many, the fight has taken on a deeply personal meaning. It's no longer just about pensions it's about reclaiming dignity, demanding recognition, and ensuring that their struggles were not in vain.

A Look at What Has Been Won and What Is Still Left to Achieve

The WASPI campaign has already left an indelible mark on British society. It has sparked a national conversation about gender, fairness, and the role of government in protecting its citizens. It has empowered thousands of women to speak out, share their stories, and demand justice.

But the work is far from complete. The fight for compensation continues, as does the broader push for systemic reform. The WASPI women know that change rarely comes quickly or easily but they also know that their voices, united, are impossible to ignore.

As the movement looks to the future, it carries with it the lessons of the past. It is a story of hope, resilience, and solidarity a story that will inspire generations to come.

Conclusion

A Story of Injustice and Perseverance: What We Can Learn from the WASPI Women The room was still, the silence punctuated only by the occasional rustle of paper or the muffled hum of the heating system. At the front, an older woman stood, her voice steady despite the weight of the words she carried. Her hands clutched a stack of petitions pages and pages filled with signatures, each one representing a story of loss, resilience, and unwavering determination.She glanced at the audience before her, a gathering of WASPI women and their supporters. Some were wiping tears from their cheeks, others sat stoically, their expressions hardened by years of struggle. But there was an unspoken bond between them, a sense of shared purpose that transcended the individual pain each woman had endured.

It was here, in moments like these, that the true essence of the WASPI campaign came alive. This was more than a fight for compensation it was a fight for recognition, dignity, and

The WASPI story is not just about a single group of women or a specific policy failure. It is a reflection of deeper systemic issues that affect societiesworldwide inequality, miscommunication, and the marginalization of certain groups.

One of the most striking lessons of the WASPI campaign is the power of collective action. The women who came together under the WASPI banner were not politicians or activists by trade. They were ordinary people teachers, nurses, caregivers, and factory workers bound by a shared injustice. Yet, their determination to be heard transformed them into a powerful movement that captured national and international attention.

Their journey illustrates the importance of standing together in the face of adversity. In a world where individual struggles can often feel isolating, the WASPI women found strength in solidarity. They proved that even the most daunting challenges can be tackled when people come together with a common purpose.

For the women born in the 1950s, the changes to the state pension age were more than just an administrative oversight they were a life-altering betrayal. Many of these women had spent decades working, raising families, and contributing to society, only to find themselves blindsided by changes that left them without the financial security they had planned for.

The emotional toll of this injustice cannot be overstated. Women who had lived stable, productive lives were suddenly thrust into uncertainty, forced to make impossible choices between paying bills, buying food, or keeping a roof over their heads. The psychological impact feelings of betrayal, anger, and despair lingered long after the initial shock.

Their stories serve as a stark reminder of the human cost of policy decisions. Behind every statistic and headline are real people, each with a unique story and a lifetime of experiences. The WASPI campaign forced society to confront these human stories, making it impossible to ignore the suffering caused by the pension changes.

Resilience in the Face of Adversity
Despite the immense challenges they faced, the WASPI women refused to give up. Their resilience is one of the defining features of their campaign, a testament to their strength and determination.

Take Linda, for example, a former nurse who had dedicated her life to caring for others. When the pension changes left her struggling to make ends meet, she could have easily succumbed to despair. Instead, she became one of the most vocal members of her local WASPI group, organizing rallies and speaking at public events.

"I wasn't just fighting for myself," she explained. "I was fighting for all of us, for every woman who had been treated unfairly."

Linda's story is just one of many. Across the country, women like her turned their anger into action, channeling their frustration into a movement that demanded change. Their courage and determination inspired others to join the fight, creating a ripple effect that extended far beyond the original group of campaigners.

What the Future Holds
As the WASPI campaign continues, its impact is already being felt in ways both tangible and intangible. While the fight for compensation is ongoing, the movement has achieved significant victories in raising awareness and pushing for greater accountability in policymaking.

Perhaps more importantly, the WASPI women have left a lasting legacy of empowerment. Their campaign has shown that even in the face of systemic injustice, it is possible to make a difference. Their stories serve as a source of inspiration for future generations, a reminder that progress is possible when people refuse to stay silent.

But there is still much work to be done. The fight for pension equality is far from over, and the broader issues of systemic inequality and economic injustice remain unresolved. The WASPI women know this better than anyone, and they are determined to continue their fight until justice is served.

A Call to Action
The story of the WASPI women is a call to action for all of us. It challenges us to question the systems and structures that govern our lives and to demand greater fairness and accountability.

It is a reminder that no one is powerless in the face of injustice. Whether through joining a campaign, signing a petition, or simply sharing a story, we all have the ability to make our voices heard.

As the WASPI movement has shown, change begins with ordinary people who refuse to accept the status quo. It begins with courage, determination, and a willingness to stand up for what is right.

The WASPI women may not have set out to change the world, but their story has become a powerful testament to the resilience of the human spirit. Their fight for justice is a story of perseverance, solidarity, and hope a story that will continue to inspire for generations to come.

As the final pages of this book close, their voices echo in the hearts of those who have read their stories. They remind us that justice is worth fighting for, that resilience is a force to be reckoned with, and that even in the darkest of times, hope can light the way forward.

Let their legacy guide us as we work toward a more just and equitable world.